GIRLS LOVE BAD GUY OVER <u>GOOD ONE</u>

DIPAN KUMAR DAS

SUDIP KUMAR DAS

To all those who have embarked on the exhilarating and sometimes tumultuous journey of love, who have explored the mysteries of romantic attraction, and who have embraced the complexities of the heart with courage and curiosity. May your own love stories be filled with understanding, growth, and the profound beauty of human connection.

Foreword

In the world of human emotions and relationships, few topics are as captivating and enigmatic as the nature of romantic attraction. It's a realm where the heart often takes the lead, guiding us through the intricate dance of love, desire, and connection. In this exploration, we delve into the complex dynamics of why some individuals are drawn to bad boys over good ones.

Romantic attraction is a deeply personal and multifaceted phenomenon, shaped by a myriad of factors including personal experiences, cultural influences, values, and innate desires. The choice of a romantic partner is a unique journey for each individual, reflecting their own narrative and aspirations.

Throughout the chapters that follow, we examine various facets of the allure of bad boys: the thrill of danger, the excitement of unpredictability, the magnetism of confidence, the illusion of change, and the intriguing dynamics found in detective love stories. As we navigate these themes, we aim to shed light on the complexities that underlie the choices individuals make in matters of the heart.

It's important to remember that while we explore these aspects, there's no universal explanation for romantic preferences. What one person finds irresistible, another may find unappealing. Ultimately, the heart's journey is a deeply personal one, and the path to love is as unique as each person who embarks upon it.

As we embark on this exploration, let us keep in mind the complexity and diversity of human emotions and relationships. May it provide insights and provoke thought, reminding us that the world of romantic attraction is a rich tapestry of emotions, desires, and experiences waiting to be unravelled.

Preface

The world of romantic attraction has long been a subject of fascination, inquiry, and artistic exploration. It's a realm where emotions run deep, where connections are forged, and where the heart often leads us into the unknown. This preface serves as an introduction to our exploration of a particular facet of romantic attraction: the allure of bad boys over good ones.

In this book, we aim to delve into the complexities that surround this intriguing phenomenon. We'll explore the various reasons why some individuals are irresistibly drawn to the bad boy archetype, examining the psychology, emotions, and narratives that underlie this attraction.

It's important to note that while we offer insights and analysis, romantic attraction is a deeply personal and multifaceted experience. There are no definitive answers or one-size-fits-all explanations. What we hope to achieve is a better understanding of the intricate dynamics at play when it comes to the preference for bad boys in matters of the heart.

Throughout the following chapters, we'll navigate the terrain of romantic attraction with an open mind and a commitment to exploring the nuances of human desire and connection. We invite you to join us on this journey, to consider the complexities of love and attraction, and to reflect on the ever-evolving landscape of human relationships.

As we embark on this exploration, let us keep in mind that the heart is a vast and enigmatic territory, and the choices we make in matters of love are as unique as the individuals who make them.

Prologue

In the grand tapestry of human emotions and relationships, few threads are as complex and enthralling as the one that weaves through the realm of romantic attraction. It's a thread that pulls us toward others, draws us into the dance of intimacy, and often leads us down unforeseen paths.

In this prologue, we set the stage for our exploration of a particular facet of romantic attraction: the enduring allure of bad boys over good ones. This journey takes us into the hearts and minds of those who find themselves irresistibly drawn to enigmatic, unpredictable, and sometimes unconventional partners.

As we embark on this exploration, we recognize that love and attraction are deeply personal, influenced by an array of factors, including past experiences, cultural influences, and individual desires. What captivates one person may leave another unmoved, and the complexities of the heart defy easy explanations.

Throughout the chapters that follow, we will navigate the intricate terrain of romantic attraction with curiosity and empathy. We will explore the psychology, emotions, and narratives that underlie the preference for bad boys, all while acknowledging that the human heart is a realm of boundless mystery and diversity.

Our aim is not to offer definitive answers but to provoke thought, spark conversation, and deepen our understanding of the multifaceted nature of romantic attraction. Together, let us embark on this journey into the realm of the heart, where the choices we make in matters of love are as unique and diverse as the individuals who make them.

CHAPTER ONE
The Allure of the Bad Boy

It's a timeless fascination, a phenomenon that has intrigued both romantics and psychologists alike - the inexplicable attraction that many girls have towards bad boys over their good counterparts. The allure of the bad boy is a puzzle that has persisted throughout the ages, leaving us to wonder what makes these seemingly troublesome individuals so irresistibly appealing.

To begin unraveling this enigma, let's explore the various facets of the bad boy mystique, starting with the primal attraction to danger. Human beings have a long history of being drawn to risky endeavors and thrilling experiences. It's a part of our nature, deeply ingrained in our evolutionary past. Bad boys often embody this essence of danger, pushing boundaries and living on the edge. This dangerous allure can be irresistible, offering an escape from the monotony of everyday life and injecting excitement into a girl's world.

The bad boy mystique also often incorporates an air of rebellion. In a society that places great emphasis on conformity and following the rules, rebels stand out. They challenge the status quo, and their non-conformity can be seen as an act of defiance. This rebellion can be appealing to girls who may feel constrained by societal norms or simply crave the thrill of breaking free from them. The bad boy represents the antithesis of the "good boy," who plays by the rules and follows a predictable path.

Beyond the thrill of danger and rebellion, there's an element of confidence and self-assuredness that sets bad boys apart. They walk with a swagger, exuding an air of self-confidence that can be magnetic. This self-assuredness can be incredibly reassuring for girls, making them feel protected and secure in the presence of someone who appears capable of handling any situation. Confidence is an attractive trait, and the bad boy often possesses it in abundance.

Furthermore, the appeal of the bad boy lies in the mystery that surrounds him. He doesn't reveal everything about himself right away; he keeps his cards close to his chest. This aura of mystery can be intoxicating. Girls often find themselves intrigued by the idea of unraveling the layers of complexity that shroud the bad boy's persona, hoping to discover the real person beneath the tough exterior.

In this chapter, we've barely scratched the surface of the intricate allure of the bad boy. This phenomenon is deeply rooted in psychology, encompassing a wide range of emotions, desires, and experiences. While some may see the attraction to bad boys as reckless, it's important to recognize that human relationships are multifaceted, and what draws one person to another is often complex and deeply personal. In the following chapters, we will continue to explore the psychology behind this attraction, delving deeper into the factors that contribute to the enduring allure of the bad boy.

Here are some examples of movies, books, and songs that explore the theme of girls being attracted to bad boys:

Movies:

"Grease" (1978): In this classic musical film, good girl Sandy falls for the rebellious bad boy, Danny Zuko, at Rydell High. The movie explores the dynamics of their relationship as they navigate the contrasting worlds of "good" and "bad."

"Twilight" series (2008-2012): The Twilight series, both in books and movies, centers around the romance between Bella Swan, a quiet and bookish girl, and Edward Cullen, a vampire with a dark and dangerous side. Edward's dangerous nature adds an element of excitement to their love story.

"The Notebook" (2004): While not a traditional "bad boy," Noah

Calhoun's working-class background and rebellious spirit make him an unlikely match for the upper-class Allie Hamilton. Their love story in "The Notebook" is a testament to the idea that love often transcends societal expectations.

Books:

"Pride and Prejudice" by Jane Austen: In this classic novel, the headstrong Elizabeth Bennet initially perceives the wealthy and aloof Mr. Darcy as a proud and disdainful man. However, as the story unfolds, she discovers his true nature, leading to a complex romance that challenges societal norms.

"Wuthering Heights" by Emily Brontë: The novel features the intense and tumultuous love between Catherine Earnshaw and Heathcliff, who is often considered a dark and brooding "bad boy" character. Their passionate and destructive relationship is central to the story.

"The Catcher in the Rye" by J.D. Salinger: Holden Caulfield, the protagonist of this iconic novel, is often seen as a rebellious and troubled character. His troubled nature and unconventional outlook on life are part of what makes him intriguing to readers.

Songs:

"Bad Guy" by Billie Eilish: This song's lyrics playfully explore the idea of a girl being attracted to a guy who presents himself as a "bad guy." The song's popularity speaks to the fascination with this concept in contemporary culture.

"I Kissed a Girl" by Katy Perry: In this song, Katy Perry sings about a girl who kisses another girl out of curiosity, hinting at the allure of exploring one's rebellious and adventurous side.

"Don't Let Me Get Me" by Pink: In this song, Pink reflects on her own struggles with self-identity and the desire to be someone she's not. The lyrics touch on the idea of girls being drawn to the idea of breaking free from societal expectations.

Movies:

"Rebel Without a Cause" (1955): This iconic film stars James Dean as Jim Stark, a troubled and rebellious teenager who catches the attention of a good girl named Judy. The movie explores the dangerous allure of Jim's character.

"Crazy, Stupid, Love" (2011): The film tells the story of Cal Weaver, a man who undergoes a transformation with the help of a charismatic womanizer, Jacob Palmer. Jacob's "bad boy" charm serves as a contrast to Cal's more conventional approach to life and relationships.

"Dirty Dancing" (1987): Frances "Baby" Houseman falls for the dance instructor Johnny Castle, who has a reputation as a bit of a ladies‘ man. The film portrays the excitement and challenges of their relationship during a summer at a resort.

Books:

"Gone Girl" by Gillian Flynn: This psychological thriller features the complex relationship between Nick and Amy Dunne. Amy’s character has elements of unpredictability and a darker side that contribute to the intrigue of their marriage.

"The Girl with the Dragon Tattoo" by Stieg Larsson: Lisbeth Salander, the enigmatic and rebellious hacker, is a central character in this gripping novel. Her unconventional nature and complex personality make her a captivating character in the story.

"The Great Gatsby" by F. Scott Fitzgerald: Jay Gatsby is a mysterious and wealthy figure with a questionable past who becomes infatuated with Daisy Buchanan, a married woman. The novel explores themes of love, wealth, and social status, with Gatsby representing a "bad boy" allure.

Songs:

"Toxic" by Britney Spears: In this song, Britney Spears sings about the intoxicating attraction to a person who is irresistible but ultimately bad for her. The lyrics capture the idea of being drawn to danger.

"Black Magic Woman" by Santana: This song is about a woman who possesses a captivating and almost mystical allure. The lyrics suggest that her enchanting nature is akin to black magic, which adds to her irresistible charm.

"Bad Romance" by Lady Gaga: Lady Gaga's song explores the complexities of romantic attraction and the idea of being drawn to a relationship that might not be good for you. The lyrics convey a sense of obsession and allure.

Movies:

"A Walk to Remember" (2002): In this film adaptation of Nicholas Sparks' novel, a good-hearted, quiet girl named Jamie falls for Landon, a troublemaker with a reputation. Their love story explores the transformational power of love and redemption.

"Moulin Rouge!" (2001): The movie features Christian, a young and idealistic writer, who becomes infatuated with Satine, a courtesan at the Moulin Rouge. Satine's daring and flirtatious persona contrasts with Christian's innocence, creating a captivating dynamic.

"The Fast and the Furious" series (2001-present): These action-packed films often revolve around the charismatic street racer Dominic Toretto, known for his "bad boy" image. His relationship with Mia, a girl from a law-abiding family, adds depth to the story.

Books:

"Beautiful Disaster" by Jamie McGuire: This novel tells the story of Abby Abernathy, a good girl, and Travis Maddox, a reckless and volatile bad boy. Their passionate and tumultuous relationship is at the heart of the story.

"Perfect Chemistry" by Simone Elkeles: The book explores the unlikely romance between Brittany Ellis, a privileged girl, and Alex Fuentes, a member of a Latino gang.

Their worlds collide, and the story delves into the complexities of their attraction.

"Fallen" by Lauren Kate: In this young adult novel, Luce Price, a girl with a mysterious past, becomes entangled with Daniel Grigori, an enigmatic and somewhat brooding character. Their connection goes beyond the ordinary and unfolds in supernatural ways.

Songs:

"I Want to Hold Your Hand" by The Beatles: This classic Beatles song expresses a desire to be close to someone, even if they might have a "bad boy" image. The song captures the universal yearning for connection.

"Burning Love" by Elvis Presley: In this song, Elvis Presley sings about a love that's like a burning fire. The intensity of the lyrics reflects the passionate and sometimes tumultuous nature of romantic attraction.

"Bad Liar" by Selena Gomez: In this song, Selena Gomez explores the theme of deception in a relationship. It hints at the idea of being attracted to someone who may not be entirely trustworthy, adding to the intrigue.

These additional examples continue to highlight the enduring fascination with the dynamic between girls and bad boys in various forms of storytelling and music. It's a theme that resonates with audiences due to its complexity and the inherent tension it brings to relationships.

It's a tale as old as time, a story that has been told and retold in countless movies, books, and songs - girls like bad boys over good ones. But why is this such a prevalent phenomenon? Is it the thrill of danger, the excitement of rebellion, or something deeper that draws women to the bad boys? In this chapter, we'll delve into the psychology behind this attraction and explore some of the reasons why girls often find themselves irresistibly drawn to the "bad boy" archetype.

The Psychology of Attraction

To understand why some girls are drawn to bad boys, we must first acknowledge that human attraction is a complex interplay of biology, psychology, and personal experiences. It's not a one-size-fits-all phenomenon, and different individuals may be attracted to different traits for various reasons. However, there are several common psychological factors that contribute to the allure of the bad boy.

1. The Thrill of Danger

One of the most prominent factors is the thrill of danger. From an evolutionary perspective, humans are wired to seek novelty and excitement. Bad boys often exude an air of unpredictability and adventure, which can be incredibly appealing. This sense of danger triggers the release of adrenaline and other neurotransmitters in the brain, creating a heightened emotional state that can be mistaken for romantic attraction.

2. The Excitement of Rebellion

Bad boys are often associated with rebellion and non-conformity, and this rebellious streak can be a powerful draw. Society places expectations and norms on individuals, and breaking free from these constraints can be liberating. Girls who may feel stifled by societal expectations may find the bad boy's willingness to defy these norms enticing.

3. Confidence and Self-Assuredness

Confidence is an attractive trait, and many bad boys exude self-assuredness. They don't seek validation from others and often project an aura of confidence that can be comforting for their partners. Girls may feel protected and secure with someone who appears capable of handling any situation, even if it means bending or breaking the rules.

4. The Element of Mystery

Bad boys often keep an element of mystery around them. They don't reveal everything about themselves immediately, leaving their partners intrigued and wanting to uncover more. This sense of mystery can be intoxicating, as girls are drawn into the challenge of unraveling the layers of complexity that shroud the bad boy's persona.

5. The Illusion of Change

Perhaps one of the most significant reasons behind the attraction to bad boys is the belief that they can be changed. Many girls are drawn to the idea of being the one who can "fix" the bad boy, to be the person who helps them leave their troubled past behind and become a better person. This desire to be a catalyst for change can be a powerful motivator in pursuing relationships with bad boys.

In conclusion, the allure of the bad boy archetype is a multifaceted phenomenon rooted in human psychology. It encompasses the thrill of danger, the excitement of rebellion, the appeal of confidence, the mystery of the unknown, and the belief in the power of transformation. These factors combine to create a compelling attraction that has been a recurring theme in literature, film, and music throughout history. However, it's essential to recognize that while some may find the bad boy allure irresistible, others may seek different qualities in their partners, and there is no one-size-fits-all explanation for romantic preferences.

CHAPTER TWO
The Bad Boy Mystique

The allure of the bad boy goes beyond simple attraction; it encompasses a mystique that captivates the imagination and beckons girls into a world of excitement and uncertainty. In this chapter, we'll dive deeper into the bad boy mystique, exploring the enigmatic qualities that make these individuals so fascinating.

The Aura of Mystery

One of the defining features of the bad boy mystique is the aura of mystery that shrouds these individuals. They don't readily share their thoughts and emotions, leaving those around them guessing about what goes on in their minds. This mysterious quality can be incredibly enticing, as it presents an ongoing challenge for those who seek to understand them.

The bad boy's reluctance to reveal their true selves gives rise to questions like: What is their backstory? What motivates them? What vulnerabilities lie beneath their tough exterior? These unanswered questions can be like a tantalizing puzzle that girls feel compelled to solve, drawing them deeper into the bad boy's world.

The Unpredictable Behavior

Bad boys are known for their unpredictable behavior, and this unpredictability is another facet of their mystique. One moment they may be aloof and distant, and the next, they could be passionately expressive. This inconsistency keeps those around them on their toes, never quite sure of what to expect next.

For many girls, this unpredictability can be thrilling. It injects an element of excitement and adventure into the relationship, preventing it from ever becoming dull or routine. The emotional rollercoaster that often accompanies the bad boy mystique can be addictive, and the anticipation of what's to come can be exhilarating.

The Rebel's Confidence

Confidence is a quality that often defines the bad boy. They exude self-assuredness and a sense of conviction in their actions. This confidence is both attractive and reassuring. Girls may feel a sense of safety and protection in the presence of someone who appears unflappable, even in the face of adversity.

The bad boy's confidence can be particularly appealing to those who crave a sense of stability in their lives. It provides a counterbalance to the chaos and unpredictability that may be part and parcel of the bad boy package. This combination of confidence and the allure of danger creates a potent mix that draws girls in.

The Irresistible Challenge

Perhaps one of the most intriguing aspects of the bad boy mystique is the challenge they present. Girls are often drawn to the idea of being the one who can break through the tough exterior and uncover the softer, more vulnerable side of the bad boy. This desire to "tame" or "change" the bad boy is a recurring theme in romantic literature and cinema.

The pursuit of this challenge can be deeply compelling. It taps into the human desire to make a difference in someone's life, to be the catalyst for transformation. The belief that they can be the one to unlock the bad boy's true potential fuels the attraction, creating a sense of purpose and meaning in the relationship.

In conclusion, the bad boy mystique is a complex and multifaceted phenomenon that encompasses mystery, unpredictability, confidence, and the allure of a challenge. It draws girls into a world of fascination, where they are both intrigued and captivated by the enigmatic qualities of these individuals. As we delve deeper into the psychology of attraction, we'll continue to unravel the layers of this intriguing dynamic and explore how it influences relationships and romantic choices.

here are some examples from literature, film, and television that illustrate the idea of the bad boy exuding an air of mystery and unpredictability:

Literature:

Heathcliff in "Wuthering Heights" by Emily Brontë: Heathcliff is the epitome of the brooding, mysterious bad boy. His dark and unpredictable nature is a central element of the novel, and it fascinates and captivates

Catherine Earnshaw and readers alike.

Jay Gatsby in "The Great Gatsby" by F. Scott Fitzgerald: Gatsby is known for his extravagant parties, mysterious past, and unrequited love for Daisy Buchanan. His enigmatic aura, combined with his wealth and reckless behavior, makes him a classic literary bad boy.

Film:

James Dean's character in "Rebel Without a Cause" (1955): James Dean's portrayal of Jim Stark epitomizes the rebellious and unpredictable bad boy. Jim is a troubled teenager who challenges authority and stands up against societal norms, adding an air of mystery to his character.

Johnny Depp as Captain Jack Sparrow in the "Pirates of the Caribbean" series: Captain Jack Sparrow is a charming and unpredictable pirate who sails by his own rules. His eccentricity, wit, and penchant for getting into and out of sticky situations create an aura of mystery and allure.

Television:

Damon Salvatore in "The Vampire Diaries": Damon is a vampire with a dark and unpredictable nature. His morally ambiguous actions and complex character development make him an enticing bad boy character throughout the series.

Spike in "Buffy the Vampire Slayer": Spike is a vampire known for his unpredictable behavior and his ability to transition between villainy and moments of surprising vulnerability. His dynamic character adds depth to the show.

Literature:

Rhett Butler in "Gone with the Wind" by Margaret Mitchell: Rhett Butler is a charismatic and enigmatic character who challenges societal norms during the American Civil War. His unpredictable actions and complicated relationship with

Scarlett O'Hara make him an enduring literary bad boy.

Holden Caulfield in "The Catcher in the Rye" by J.D. Salinger: Holden Caulfield is a rebellious and troubled teenager who defies authority and societal expectations. His unpredictable behavior and unique perspective on life contribute to the book's enduring popularity.

Film:

Tyler Durden in "Fight Club" (1999): Tyler Durden, played by Brad Pitt, is the charismatic and unpredictable leader of an underground fight club. His mysterious and anarchic nature draws the narrator (played by

Edward Norton) into a world of chaos and self-discovery.

Edward Cullen in "Twilight" series: Edward Cullen, a vampire, exudes an air of mystery and unpredictability due to his supernatural abilities and the secrecy surrounding his true nature. His attraction to Bella Swan is central to the series.

Television:

Sawyer in "Lost": Sawyer, portrayed by Josh Holloway, is a complex character known for his unpredictability and rough exterior. His mysterious past and the layers of his personality make him a compelling bad boy figure on the show.

Tony Stark (Iron Man) in the Marvel Cinematic Universe: Tony Stark, portrayed by Robert Downey Jr., is a genius inventor with a charismatic and often unpredictable personality. His playboy demeanor and occasional recklessness contribute to his bad boy image, especially in the earlier films of the franchise.

Literature:

Rhysand in "A Court of Thorns and Roses" by Sarah J. Maas: Rhysand is a High Lord of the Night Court in this fantasy series. He is known for his enigmatic personality, cunning, and complex motivations, which add depth to the romantic tension in the story.

Jay Gatsby in "The Great Gatsby" by F. Scott Fitzgerald: Gatsby is a millionaire with a mysterious background who throws extravagant parties. His allure comes from his unpredictable behavior and the enigmatic aura surrounding his wealth and social status.

Film:

John Bender in "The Breakfast Club" (1985): John Bender, portrayed by Judd Nelson, is the quintessential bad boy in this classic teen film. His rebellious and unpredictable nature clashes with the other characters during their Saturday detention.

Don Draper in "Mad Men": Don Draper, played by Jon Hamm, is a complex character in the advertising industry. His enigmatic personality and the mystery surrounding his true identity contribute to his allure and the intrigue of the series.

Television:

Klaus Mikaelson in "The Vampire Diaries" and "The Originals": Klaus, a hybrid vampire-werewolf, is known for his unpredictability, impulsiveness, and charisma. His complexity and mysterious past make him a central character in both series.

Logan Echolls in "Veronica Mars": Logan, portrayed by Jason Dohring, is a troubled and unpredictable character who undergoes significant development throughout the series.

His complex personality and the challenges he faces add depth to his character.

These additional examples showcase how the bad boy archetype, characterized by an air of mystery and unpredictability, remains a compelling and enduring element in literature, film, and television. These characters continue to captivate audiences by exploring the complexities of human nature and the allure of the unknown.

In the world of romance and attraction, few elements are as captivating as mystery. It is a force that transcends logic, pulling individuals into a realm of intrigue and fascination. In the context of bad boys and their undeniable appeal, the element of mystery plays a pivotal role. In this chapter, we'll delve deeper into how mystery functions as a powerful magnet, drawing girls toward the enigmatic world of the bad boy.

The Uncharted Territory

At the heart of the allure of mystery lies the appeal of uncharted territory. When we encounter something mysterious, we are faced with the unknown, an undiscovered country of thoughts, emotions, and experiences. Bad boys often exude an air of mystery, leaving girls to wonder what lies beneath their exterior.

The desire to explore this uncharted territory is a fundamental human drive. We are naturally curious beings, eager to uncover hidden truths and secrets. Bad boys, with their unpredictable behavior and guarded emotions, become an enticing puzzle that begs to be solved. Girls find themselves irresistibly drawn to the challenge of understanding the enigma that is the bad boy.

The Compulsion to Decode

Human beings are wired to seek patterns and make sense of the world around them. When faced with a mystery, our brains engage in a process of decoding and deciphering. This cognitive challenge is not only mentally stimulating but also emotionally rewarding. It gives us a sense of accomplishment and satisfaction when we unravel the secrets of the unknown.

Bad boys present a unique decoding challenge. They often communicate in nuances, leaving much unsaid. Their actions may seem contradictory, and their motivations are far from transparent. Girls are drawn to the idea of being the one who can decipher the bad boy's thoughts and emotions, peeling away the layers of complexity to reveal the true person beneath.

The Emotional Rollercoaster

Mystery adds an emotional depth to the attraction. The ups and downs of trying to understand a complex, mysterious individual create a rollercoaster of emotions. There's frustration when deciphering their behavior seems impossible, followed by moments of elation when a breakthrough is achieved. This emotional rollercoaster becomes a powerful bonding experience, forging a connection between the girl and the bad boy.

Moreover, the uncertainty that comes with a mysterious partner keeps the relationship exciting. It prevents it from settling into a predictable routine, as every interaction becomes an opportunity to uncover something new. This emotional intensity can be highly addictive, making it challenging to walk away from the allure of the bad boy.

The Desire for Depth

In a world where surface-level interactions abound, the desire for depth and substance in relationships is profound. Mystery often suggests hidden depths, and girls are drawn to the idea that beneath the bad boy's exterior lies a complex and multifaceted personality. They crave the depth that comes from understanding someone on a profound level.

Bad boys offer the promise of depth and complexity, making girls feel like they are embarking on a journey of discovery. This desire for depth transcends mere physical attraction and taps into the fundamental human need for meaningful connections.

In summary, the element of mystery is a powerful force in the attraction between girls and bad boys. It draws individuals into uncharted territory, compels them to decode the enigma, intensifies the emotional rollercoaster, and satisfies the desire for depth in relationships. As we continue to explore the psychology behind this attraction, we'll uncover more layers of the intricate dance between mystery and desire that fuels the allure of the bad boy.

CHAPTER THREE
Confidence and Self-Assuredness

Confidence is a quality that has the power to captivate, inspire, and, most importantly, attract. In the realm of romantic attraction, confidence and self-assuredness are often like a magnet, drawing people towards individuals who exude a sense of certainty and self-belief. In this chapter, we'll explore the role of confidence and self-assuredness in the allure of the bad boy archetype and why these traits hold such sway over those who are drawn to them.

The Magnetic Pull of Confidence

Confidence is one of those intangible qualities that, when possessed in abundance, can be utterly magnetic. The bad boy often exudes an unshakable confidence, a belief in themselves and their actions that is nothing short of captivating. This confidence is a potent force in the realm of attraction, and there are several reasons why it has such a compelling effect:

1. Confidence is Attractive: Confidence is universally considered an attractive trait. When someone is confident, it sends a signal that they are comfortable in their own skin, which is inherently appealing. It conveys a sense of self-assuredness that draws others in.

2. The Illusion of Strength: Confidence can be equated with strength. People often find themselves naturally drawn to those who appear strong and capable. The bad boy's unwavering self-assuredness can make girls feel safe and protected, as if they are with someone who can handle any situation that comes their way.

3. Confidence Breeds Trust: Confidence often goes hand in hand with trustworthiness. People tend to trust those who project confidence because they believe that such individuals are less likely to falter or betray them. This trust can form the foundation of strong emotional connections.

4. A Sense of Control: Confidence can also convey a sense of control and agency. The bad boy's ability to take charge and make decisions with conviction can be reassuring to those who may be seeking a partner who can lead and provide direction.

The Confidence Paradox

One intriguing aspect of the bad boy's confidence is that it can coexist with traits that, in other contexts, might be considered less than virtuous. This creates a paradox where individuals may be attracted to the very qualities that, under different circumstances, they would deem undesirable. For example, the bad boy's confidence may be accompanied by traits like rebelliousness, impulsivity, or even arrogance.

The allure lies in the perception that the bad boy is unapologetically himself, without the need for external validation or conformity to societal norms. It's as if the bad boy has figured something out—a secret to living life on their own terms—and this confidence in their own path is irresistible.

The Reassurance of Confidence

Confidence can provide reassurance and a sense of stability in the tumultuous world of romantic relationships. The bad boy's confidence can make girls feel as though they are with someone who can weather the storms of life and provide a steady anchor. This reassurance can be particularly appealing to those who may have experienced uncertainty or instability in the past.

In conclusion, confidence and self-assuredness are key elements of the allure of the bad boy archetype. The unwavering belief in oneself, the magnetic pull of confidence, and the sense of strength and control it conveys create a compelling attraction. However, it's essential to recognize that confidence alone does not define a person's character, and the pursuit of balanced, healthy relationships should always be the ultimate goal. As we continue our exploration of the psychology behind the bad boy allure, we'll uncover more layers of this complex dynamic.

here are some examples from literature, film, and television that illustrate the role of confidence in the bad boy allure and why it can be such a potent magnet for women:

Literature:

Christian Grey in "Fifty Shades of Grey" by E.L. James: Christian Grey is a wealthy and dominant character who exudes confidence and self-assuredness. His unwavering demeanor and control over his life are central to his appeal, even though his character exhibits complex and controversial traits.

Mr. Rochester in "Jane Eyre" by Charlotte Brontë: Mr. Rochester is a classic literary character known for his strong and sometimes brooding personality. His confidence and assertiveness play a significant role in his relationship with Jane Eyre, drawing her to him despite his mysterious past.

Film:

James Bond in the "James Bond" film series: James Bond, portrayed by various actors over the years, is the quintessential confident and suave character. His self-assured demeanor, charisma, and ability to handle high-pressure situations make him an enduring symbol of masculine confidence.

Tony Stark (Iron Man) in the Marvel Cinematic Universe: Tony Stark, portrayed by Robert Downey Jr., is a billionaire genius inventor known for his charisma and self-confidence. His unwavering belief in himself and his ability to take charge of challenging situations are central to his character's appeal.

Television:

Don Draper in "Mad Men": Don Draper, played by Jon Hamm, is a confident and enigmatic character in the advertising industry. His self-assuredness in the boardroom and his complex persona contribute to his allure, despite his flaws and complexities.

Spike in "Buffy the Vampire Slayer": Spike, portrayed by James Marsters, is a vampire known for his swagger and self-confidence. His confident and unapologetic nature, combined with his unpredictable behavior, adds to his appeal in the series.

Real-Life Examples:

James Dean: The iconic actor James Dean was known for his rebellious and confident persona both on and off the screen. His self-assuredness and non-conformity made him a symbol of youthful confidence in the 1950s.

Elon Musk: Elon Musk, the entrepreneur and CEO of companies like Tesla and SpaceX, is known for his unwavering confidence in his vision for the future of technology and space exploration. His self-assuredness and determination have garnered admiration from many.

James Bond in the "James Bond" film series: James Bond, known as Agent 007, is a fictional character created by author Ian Fleming. He's a British secret service agent known for his confidence, charisma, and ability to handle high-stakes situations with ease. Here's how confidence plays a significant role in his appeal:

Unwavering Self-Assuredness: James Bond is the epitome of self-assuredness. Whether he's facing a dangerous villain or seducing an enemy agent, his unshakable confidence is evident. This confidence is deeply appealing because it conveys the message that he is in control and can handle any challenge that comes his way.

Charisma: Bond's confidence is accompanied by charisma, making him an engaging and charming character. He knows how to navigate social situations effortlessly, whether it's at a high-stakes poker game or a glamorous party. His ability to exude confidence and charm draws both allies and adversaries to him.

Fearlessness: Bond's confidence is also reflected in his fearlessness. He takes risks, confronts danger head-on, and remains composed under pressure. This fearlessness adds an element of excitement and adventure to his character, which can be highly attractive to those drawn to the thrill of danger.

Problem Solving: Bond's confidence extends to his problem-solving abilities. He approaches challenges with a cool and collected demeanor, analyzing situations and making quick decisions. His ability to think on his feet and devise creative solutions showcases his self-assuredness and competence.

Elon Musk: Elon Musk is a real-life entrepreneur and CEO known for his confidence in pursuing ambitious goals in the fields of electric vehicles, space exploration, and renewable energy. His confidence is evident in his public persona and business ventures:

Visionary Confidence: Musk's confidence is rooted in his visionary outlook on the future. He believes in the potential of groundbreaking technologies and is unafraid to invest his resources and reputation in pursuing them. This unwavering belief in his vision is attractive because it demonstrates a bold and pioneering spirit.

Resilience: Musk's confidence is also reflected in his resilience in the face of adversity. He has faced numerous challenges and setbacks in his career but has consistently persevered and maintained his self-assuredness. This resilience can be inspiring and reassuring to others.

Leadership: Musk's confidence in his leadership abilities is evident in his role as CEO of multiple companies. His willingness to take charge of complex projects, set ambitious goals, and guide teams toward achieving them is a testament to his confidence in his abilities.

Innovation: Musk's confidence is linked to his willingness to challenge the status quo and push the boundaries of technology. This innovative spirit, combined with his confidence, has resulted in groundbreaking advancements in electric vehicles, space exploration, and renewable energy.

In both characters like James Bond and real-life figures like Elon Musk, confidence plays a central role in their appeal. It conveys a sense of self-assuredness, competence, and the ability to navigate challenges with grace. This confidence can be deeply attractive, as it provides a sense of security, leadership, and the promise of a bold and exciting journey. For many, these qualities make individuals like James Bond and Elon Musk magnetic figures, whether on the silver screen or in real life.

CHAPTER FOUR

The Excitement of the Unpredictable

In the realm of romantic attraction, few things rival the exhilaration of unpredictability. The bad boy, with his penchant for defying conventions and living life on his terms, embodies this sense of excitement and uncertainty. In this chapter, we'll explore why the unpredictability of the bad boy is such a magnetic force, drawing women into a world of thrill and adventure.

The Appeal of Unconventionality

The bad boy is often the antithesis of predictability and conformity. He doesn't adhere to societal norms, doesn't always play by the rules, and embraces a lifestyle that is outside the boundaries of convention. This unconventional approach to life can be profoundly appealing for several reasons:

1. Freedom from Routine: Predictability and routine can sometimes feel stifling. The bad boy represents an escape from the mundane and a departure from the ordinary. His willingness to break free from the shackles of routine offers the promise of excitement and adventure.

2. A Taste of Rebellion: Humans have a natural inclination to rebel against authority and restrictions. The bad boy embodies this spirit of rebellion, standing up against the establishment and defying societal expectations. His rebellion can be contagious, inviting others to join in the thrill of breaking the rules.

3. Escaping the Comfort Zone: Unpredictability challenges individuals to step out of their comfort zones. It forces them to confront the unknown and adapt to changing circumstances. This challenge can be invigorating, as it pushes people to grow and discover new facets of themselves.

The Adrenaline Rush

Unpredictability often goes hand in hand with excitement and the rush of adrenaline. The bad boy's willingness to take risks and embrace the unexpected creates an environment where every moment is charged with the potential for adventure. This adrenaline rush can be incredibly enticing for several reasons:

1. Emotional Intensity: Unpredictable situations often lead to heightened emotional experiences. The rollercoaster of emotions, from exhilaration to uncertainty, can be deeply engaging. It makes individuals feel alive and fully immersed in the present moment.

2. Thrill-Seeking: Some people are naturally drawn to thrill-seeking experiences. The bad boy's lifestyle, filled with unexpected twists and turns, provides ample opportunities for those seeking excitement and adventure.

3. The Element of Surprise: Unpredictability introduces an element of surprise into relationships. It keeps things fresh and prevents them from becoming stagnant. This element of surprise can be particularly alluring, as it adds an air of spontaneity and novelty to the relationship.

The Complexity of the Unpredictable

The unpredictable nature of the bad boy also adds layers of complexity to his character. This complexity can be intellectually stimulating and emotionally rewarding for those who are drawn to him. Here's why:

1. Intellectual Challenge: Trying to understand the bad boy's motivations and decipher his behavior can be intellectually challenging. It requires individuals to think critically and engage their minds in unraveling the mysteries surrounding him.

2. Emotional Depth: Unpredictability often leads to moments of vulnerability and authenticity. The bad boy's complex personality may reveal moments of tenderness and

depth that are unexpected but profoundly touching.

3. The Potential for Change: Many are drawn to the idea that they can be the one to change the bad boy, to be the catalyst for transformation in his life. This desire to unlock his potential and witness growth can be a powerful motivator.

In conclusion, the unpredictability of the bad boy is a potent magnet for women because it offers an escape from routine, a taste of rebellion, and an adrenaline-fueled journey. It challenges individuals to step out of their comfort zones, provides an emotional rollercoaster, and adds layers of complexity to the relationship. The allure of unpredictability taps into the human desire for excitement, adventure, and the thrill of the unknown, making the bad boy an irresistible figure in the realm of romantic attraction.

In the world of detective love stories, the contrast between the unpredictable bad boy and the dependable, "good" counterpart often serves as a compelling narrative device. These stories explore how the thrill of the unpredictable can make bad boys seem more appealing, even in the context of solving mysteries and pursuing justice. In this chapter, we'll delve into the dynamics of detective love stories and how they highlight the allure of unpredictability.

The Enigmatic Detective

Detective love stories frequently feature a lead character who is a skilled investigator but also embodies elements of the bad boy archetype. This detective is characterized by their:

1. Unconventional Methods: The detective often employs unconventional and sometimes morally ambiguous methods to solve cases. They may bend or break the rules, which adds an element of unpredictability to their approach.

2. Mysterious Past: Many detective characters have a mysterious past, often involving a troubled history or unresolved personal issues. This

enigmatic backstory contributes to their allure and unpredictability.

3. Complex Personality: These detectives are rarely one-dimensional. They have complex personalities that include vulnerabilities, inner conflicts, and hidden depths. This complexity makes them fascinating and unpredictable.

The Dependable Partner

On the other side of the equation, there is often a "good" counterpart—a partner, colleague, or love interest—who represents stability, reliability, and a commitment to justice through conventional means. This character:

1. Follows the Rules: The dependable partner adheres to the law and ethical principles. They are committed to solving cases through legal and conventional investigative methods.

2. Provides Stability: This character often offers stability and emotional support to the unpredictable detective. They can be seen as a moral compass, guiding the detective toward ethical decisions.

3. Offers Emotional Connection: The dependable partner may establish a strong emotional connection with the unpredictable detective. Their relationship often involves a dynamic of tension and attraction.

The Allure of Unpredictability

Detective love stories capitalize on the allure of unpredictability in several ways:

1. Tension and Chemistry: The contrast between the unpredictable detective and the dependable partner creates tension and chemistry that keeps audiences engaged. The unpredictability of the detective's actions adds excitement to the narrative.

2. Intellectual Challenge: The process of solving mysteries in unconventional ways adds an intellectual challenge to the story. Audiences are drawn into the detective's world, where they must decipher the logic behind the unpredictable methods.

3. Emotional Rollercoaster: The unpredictable detective's complex personality and mysterious past create an emotional rollercoaster. The audience experiences a range of emotions, from frustration to empathy, as they uncover the layers of the character's psyche.

4. Transformation and Redemption: Detective love stories often explore themes of transformation and redemption. The unpredictable detective may undergo character development and growth, making their journey from unpredictability to stability a central element of the narrative.

In these stories, the allure of unpredictability is portrayed as a double-edged sword. While the unpredictable bad boy detective may be captivating and exciting, their actions can also lead to moral dilemmas and conflicts. The dependable partner represents a stabilizing force, but their commitment to following the rules can be seen as predictable and lacking in adventure.

Ultimately, detective love stories provide a platform to explore the complex interplay between the unpredictable and the predictable in romantic attraction. They highlight how the thrill of the unpredictable can make bad boys seem more appealing, even in the context of solving mysteries and pursuing justice.

here's a short unpredictable love story:

Title: "The Uncharted Journey"

Sarah had always been a planner. Her life was meticulously organized, from her career to her daily routine. But when she met Luke, everything changed.

Luke was the complete opposite of Sarah. He was spontaneous, unpredictable, and had an insatiable thirst for adventure. They met during a hiking trip in the rugged mountains, where Sarah had gone to escape the monotony of her daily life.

Their connection was instant and electric. Sarah found herself drawn to Luke's carefree spirit, while Luke admired Sarah's intelligence and determination. They decided to embark on a journey together, not knowing where it would lead.

They traveled to far-off places, explored hidden gems, and embraced the thrill of spontaneity. Each day was an adventure, and they reveled in the unpredictability of their new life together.

One day, while hiking through a dense forest, they stumbled upon an old cabin. Inside, they discovered a collection of handwritten letters dating back decades. As they read the letters, they uncovered a love story that was just as unpredictable as their own.

The letters told the tale of Eleanor and James, two souls who had also chosen the path less traveled. They had met during a cross-country road trip and had fallen in love, despite the odds stacked against them. Their love had been filled with surprises and challenges, but it had endured.

Inspired by Eleanor and James's story, Sarah and Luke decided to leave their own mark on the cabin. They penned a letter to each other, expressing their love and gratitude for the unpredictable journey they were on.

Years later, when they revisited the cabin, they found their letter and realized that their love had grown deeper and more enduring with each twist and turn of their unpredictable adventure.

In the end, Sarah had learned that life's greatest moments often occurred when you let go of the need for control and embraced the unpredictability of the journey. Luke had shown her that sometimes, the most beautiful love stories were the ones that couldn't be planned. Together, they had found a love that was both wild and unpredictable, and they wouldn't have it any other way.

CHAPTER FIVE

The Illusion of Change

In the realm of romantic attraction, one of the alluring aspects of the bad boy archetype is the tantalizing prospect of change. The belief that one can transform a wayward soul into a better, more virtuous person can be a potent magnet for women. In this chapter, we'll explore the allure of the illusion of change and why it plays a significant role in the appeal of bad boys.

The Appeal of Redemption

The bad boy often carries a sense of mystery and darkness, and this very darkness can be what draws women in. There's an innate desire to believe in the power of love and redemption, to be the one who can unravel the layers of complexity and lead the bad boy toward a path of goodness. This appeal of redemption is rooted in several factors:

1. The Heroic Fantasy: Many individuals harbor a heroic fantasy deep within them. They yearn to be the hero or heroine who saves

someone from their troubled past and helps them find their way to a better future. The bad boy offers an opportunity to fulfill this fantasy.

2. Emotional Investment: As humans, we tend to become emotionally invested in our relationships. When women are drawn to bad boys, they invest their emotions and energies into the belief that their love and influence can bring about positive change. This emotional investment becomes a driving force in the relationship.

3. The Challenge of Transformation: The idea of changing someone with a troubled past can be seen as a noble and admirable challenge. It's a test of one's love and commitment, and

many are drawn to the idea of overcoming obstacles together and forging a deeper connection through transformation.

The Illusion of Control

The allure of the illusion of change is closely tied to the notion of control. Women who are drawn to bad boys may believe that they have the power to influence and guide the bad boy's choices, ultimately leading him down a better path. This illusion of control can be captivating for several reasons:

1. Empowerment: The belief that one can change another person empowers individuals. It makes them feel as though they have agency and

influence over their partner's life, which can be gratifying.

2. Emotional Investment: The more emotionally invested one becomes in the relationship, the stronger the desire to believe in the possibility of change. This emotional investment can make individuals more willing to overlook the bad boy's flaws and focus on their potential for transformation.

3. Validation of Love: Successfully changing a bad boy may be seen as validation of one's love and commitment. It confirms that their love was strong enough to inspire positive change, and this validation can be deeply rewarding.

The Reality of Change

While the illusion of change can be a powerful force, it's essential to acknowledge its limitations. Change is a complex and often gradual process that requires the active participation and willingness of the person undergoing transformation. The bad boy's desire and motivation to change must come from within, rather than solely as a result of a partner's influence.

In some cases, the belief in the power of love to change a person can lead to disappointment and heartache when the bad boy's transformation doesn't align with expectations. However, the journey of attempting to change someone can also be a valuable learning experience, fostering personal growth and self-discovery.

In conclusion, the allure of the illusion of change is a significant factor in the appeal of bad boys. The belief in redemption, the heroic fantasy, and the illusion of control all contribute to the captivating power of this dynamic. While change is possible, it's essential to approach relationships with a realistic understanding of the complexities involved and the need for genuine willingness on the part of the individual undergoing transformation.

here are a few examples from literature, film, and television where women are drawn to bad boys with the belief that they can change them:

Literature:

Scarlett O'Hara in "Gone with the Wind" by Margaret Mitchell: Scarlett is initially drawn to the roguish Rhett Butler, who is considered a bad boy. She believes that she can change him and make him love her, despite his reputation for being unpredictable and unconventional.

Tessa Gray in "The Infernal Devices" series by Cassandra Clare: Tessa's relationship with Will Herondale, a brooding and mysterious character, is marked by her belief that she can help him overcome his inner demons and change his self-destructive behavior.

Film:

Sandy Olsson in "Grease" (1978): In this musical film, Sandy falls for Danny Zuko, the quintessential bad boy. Throughout the movie, she believes she can change him and turn him into a more caring and responsible partner.

Baby Houseman in "Dirty Dancing" (1987): Baby is initially attracted to Johnny Castle, a rebellious dance instructor with a questionable reputation. She believes she can change him and help him escape the limitations of his circumstances.

Television:

Buffy Summers in "Buffy the Vampire Slayer": Buffy, the titular character, is drawn to the vampire Spike, a character with a dark and violent past. Throughout the series, she believes she can inspire him to change and choose a more virtuous path.

Elena Gilbert in "The Vampire Diaries": Elena is initially attracted to the vampire Damon Salvatore, who has a history of unpredictability and violence. She believes she can redeem him and guide him toward better choices.

Literature:

Isabella Swan in "Twilight" by Stephenie Meyer: Bella is attracted to

Edward Cullen, a vampire with a mysterious and dangerous side. She believes that her love can help him resist his vampire instincts and live a more human life.

Anna Karenina in "Anna Karenina" by Leo Tolstoy: Anna becomes involved with Count Alexei Vronsky, a charming but reckless officer. She believes that her love can change his behavior and lead to a more stable life together.

Film:

Annie Hall in "Annie Hall" (1977): In this classic Woody Allen film, Annie Hall falls for Alvy Singer, a neurotic comedian with a penchant for self-destructive behavior. She initially believes she can change him, but their relationship faces challenges due to their differences.

Rose DeWitt Bukater in "Titanic" (1997): Rose, a young socialite, falls in love with Jack Dawson, an artist from a lower social class. Her belief in their love transcending class boundaries and changing their fates is central to the film's narrative.

Television:

Olivia Pope in "Scandal": Olivia, a skilled crisis manager, has a complicated relationship with Fitzgerald "Fitz" Grant, the President of the United States. She believes that her influence can help him make better decisions and lead the country in a more ethical direction.

Pam Beesly in "The Office": Pam is initially engaged to Roy Anderson, a warehouse worker with a volatile temper. She later develops feelings for Jim Halpert, a co-worker known for his pranks and unpredictability. Pam's belief in her connection with Jim leads her to leave Roy and pursue a relationship with Jim.

Literature:

Juliet Capulet in "Romeo and Juliet" by William Shakespeare: Juliet falls in love with Romeo, a member of a rival family known for their feuding. She believes their love can bridge the gap between their families and bring about change in their society.

Elizabeth Bennet in "Pride and Prejudice" by Jane Austen: Elizabeth is initially wary of Mr. Darcy's reserved and aloof demeanor. However, as she gets to know him better, she believes that her influence can encourage him to become a more open and caring person.

Film:

Hermione Granger in the "Harry Potter" series: Hermione becomes romantically involved with Ron Weasley, who is known for his mischievous and impulsive behavior. She believes that her support and influence can help him mature and become a more responsible wizard.

Allie Hamilton in "The Notebook" (2004): Allie falls in love with Noah Calhoun, a passionate but working-class man. Despite her family's objections, she believes that their love can transcend social and economic barriers.

Television:

Rachel Green in "Friends": Rachel has an on-again, off-again relationship with Ross Geller, a brilliant but socially awkward paleontologist. She believes that her love and friendship can help Ross become more emotionally aware and navigate his relationships better.

Carrie Bradshaw in "Sex and the City": Carrie is infatuated with Mr. Big, a wealthy and emotionally distant businessman. Throughout the series, she believes that her love and influence can help him commit to a more serious relationship.

These examples further illustrate the enduring theme of women being drawn to bad boys with the hope of inspiring change and transformation. It reflects the belief in the power of love to shape and influence individuals, even when faced with challenges and differences.

Romantic preferences are indeed complex and deeply personal. There's no universal explanation for why some individuals are drawn to bad boys while others prefer more dependable partners. People's choices in romantic partners are influenced by a multitude of factors, including their past experiences, values, personalities, and individual desires.

Relationship dynamics are unique to each couple, and what works for one may not work for another. Some individuals may find excitement and growth in relationships with bad boys, while others may prioritize stability and reliability in their partnerships with good guys.

It's essential to recognize that there's no inherently right or wrong choice when it comes to selecting a romantic partner. What matters most is that both individuals in a relationship are happy, fulfilled, and feel supported in their journey together. Ultimately, love and attraction are profoundly subjective experiences, and the path to finding a compatible partner varies from person to person.

Epilogue

In the exploration of why some individuals are drawn to bad boys over good ones, we've uncovered a tapestry of human desires, emotions, and complexities. Love and romantic attraction are among the most intricate aspects of the human experience, defying easy explanations or one-size-fits-all theories.

Throughout this journey, we've touched upon various elements that contribute to the allure of bad boys: the thrill of danger, the excitement of unpredictability, the confidence and self-assuredness they exude, the illusion of change, and the intricate dynamics found in detective love stories. Yet, it's crucial to remember that these are just facets of a much broader and intricate mosaic.

In truth, every individual's romantic preferences are shaped by a unique blend of personal experiences, values, cultural influences, and innate desires. The complexities of the human heart are such that what one person finds irresistible, another may find unappealing.

It's also essential to recognize that relationships are not solely about labels like "good" or "bad" but about the deeper connections, shared experiences, and emotional bonds that two people form over time. The best relationships are built on mutual respect, trust, communication, and compatibility, regardless of whether they involve bad boys or good ones.

As we conclude our exploration, we leave you with the understanding that romantic attraction remains a beautifully enigmatic and deeply personal part of the human journey. It's a realm where the heart often guides us, defying logic and rationale. The intricacies of love are a testament to the richness of the human experience, reminding us that there's no one-size-fits-all formula for matters of the heart.

May your own journey through the complexities of romantic attraction be filled with understanding, compassion, and the deep connection that makes love a truly remarkable and transformative force in our lives.

.....***.....